KUBA

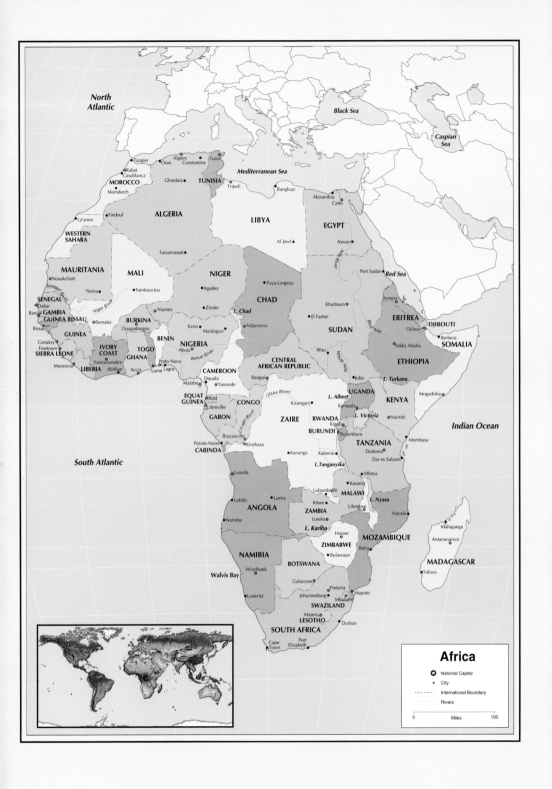

North
Atlantic

Black Sea

Caspian
Sea

Tangier
Algiers
Oran   Constantine   Tunis
Rabat
Casablanca
MOROCCO   Ghardaia   TUNISIA   Mediterranean Sea
Marrakech   Tripoli   Banghazi
Alexandria
Cairo
La'youn   ALGERIA   LIBYA   EGYPT
WESTERN   Tindouf
SAHARA
Tamanrasset   Al Jawf   Aswan

MAURITANIA   MALI   NIGER   Faya-Largeau   Port Sudan   Red Sea
Nouakchott   Agadez   CHAD   Asmera
Nema   Tombouctou   Zinder   Khartoum   ERITREA
SENEGAL   Niamey   L. Chad   El Fasher   SUDAN   Djibouti   DJIBOUTI
Dakar   Niger River   Kano   Maiduguri   Ndjamena   Berbera
GAMBIA   Bamako   BURKINA   Addis Ababa   SOMALIA
GUINEA BISSAU   Ouagadougou   BENIN   Wau   Blue Nile   ETHIOPIA
Bissau   GUINEA   NIGERIA   CENTRAL   White Nile   Juba   L. Turkana
Conakry   IVORY   TOGO   Abuja   AFRICAN REPUBLIC   Mogadishu
Freetown   COAST   GHANA   Porto Novo   Benue River   Banqui
SIERRA LEONE   Yamoussoukro   Lome   Lagos   CAMEROON   UGANDA   KENYA
Monrovia   Abidjan   Accra   Douala   Yaounde   L. Albert
LIBERIA   EQUAT.   Malabo   (Zaire River)   Kisangani   L. Victoria   Nairobi   Indian Ocean
GUINEA   Bata   CONGO   ZAIRE   RWANDA   Kampala   Mombasa
Libreville   Brazzaville   Kigali   L. Victoria
GABON   Congo River   BURUNDI   Bujumbura
Pointe-Noire   Kinshasa   Kananga   Kalemie   TANZANIA   Dodoma
South Atlantic   CABINDA   Dar es Salaam
L.Tanganyika   Mbeya
Luanda   Kasama
Lobito   Luena   Lubumbashi   MALAWI   L. Nyasa   Nacala
ANGOLA   Kitwe   ZAMBIA   Lilongwe
Namibe   Lusaka   L. Kariba   Mahajanga
Harare   MOZAMBIQUE   Antananarivo
NAMIBIA   BOTSWANA   ZIMBABWE   Beira
Bulawayo   MADAGASCAR
Walvis Bay   Windhoek   Gaborone   Toliara
Luderitz   Pretoria   Maputo
Johannesburg   Mbabane
SWAZILAND
Maseru   Durban
LESOTHO
SOUTH AFRICA
Cape   Port
Town   Elizabeth

Africa

✪ National Capital
• City
- - - - International Boundary
——— Rivers

0   Miles   100

The Heritage Library of African Peoples

KUBA

Rebecca Leuchak, Ph.D.

THE ROSEN PUBLISHING GROUP, INC.
NEW YORK

Published in 1998 by The Rosen Publishing Group, Inc.
29 East 21st Street, New York, NY 10010

First Edition

Manufactured in the United States of America

Library of Congress Cataloging-in-Publication Data

Leuchak, Rebecca.
    Kuba / Rebecca Leuchak.
        p.   cm.—(The heritage library of African peoples)
    Includes bibliographical references and index.
    Summary: Surveys the history, culture, and contemporary life of
the Kuba people of central Africa.
    ISBN 0-8239-1996-X
    1. Kuba (African people)—History—Juvenile literature.   2. Kuba
(African people)—Social life and customs—Juvenile literature.
[1. Kuba (African people)]   I. Title.   II. Series.
DT650.K83L48   1997
967.5′26—dc21   97-25410
                                                                  CIP
                                                                  AC

Contents

INTRODUCTION

THERE IS EVERY REASON FOR US TO KNOW something about Africa and to understand its past and the way of life of its peoples. Africa is a rich continent that has for centuries provided the world with art, culture, labor, wealth, and natural resources. It has vast mineral deposits, fossil fuels, and commercial crops.

But perhaps most important is the fact that fossil evidence indicates that human beings originated in Africa. The earliest traces of human beings and their tools are almost two million years old. Their descendants have migrated throughout the world. To be human is to be of African descent.

The experiences of the peoples who stayed in Africa are as rich and as diverse as of those who established themselves elsewhere. This series of books describes their environment, their modes of subsistence, their relationships, and their customs and beliefs. The books present the variety of languages, histories, cultures, and religions that are to be found on the African continent. They demonstrate the historical linkages between African peoples and the way contemporary Africa has been affected by European colonial rule.

Africa is large, complex, and diverse. It encompasses an area of more than 11,700,000 square miles. The United States, Europe, and India could fit easily into it. The sheer size is an indication of the continent's great variety in geography, terrain, climate, flora, fauna, peoples, languages, and cultures.

Much of contemporary Africa has been shaped by European colonial rule, industrialization, urbanization, and the demands of a world economic system. For more than seventy years, large regions of Africa were ruled by Great Britain, France, Belgium, Portugal, and Spain. African peoples from various ethnic, linguistic, and cultural backgrounds were brought together to form colonial states.

For decades Africans struggled to gain their independence. It was not until after World War II that the colonial territories became independent African states. Today, almost all of Africa is ruled by Africans. Large numbers of Africans live in modern cities. Rural Africa is also being transformed, and yet its people still engage in many of their customs and beliefs.

Contemporary circumstances and natural events have not always been kind to ordinary Africans. Today, however, new popular social movements and technological innovations pose great promise for future development.

George C. Bond, Ph.D., Director
Institute of African Studies
Columbia University, New York

The Kuba Kingdom has a rich history covering several centuries. This noble is dressed for the 1970 state visit of the Kuba king Kot aMbweeky III.

chapter

1

THE LAND AND THE PEOPLE

THE KUBA KINGDOM HAS EXISTED FOR centuries. It has survived both the upheavals of the colonial period and the political disturbances in the Democratic Republic of the Congo (known as the Congo), which is where the Kuba live today.

The Kuba people are a union of more than twenty ethnic groups, including the Boshongo, Ngeende, Ngongo, Shoowa, Bieeng, Idiing, Ilebo, Kel, Kayuweeng, Kete, Bulaang, Pyaang, Mbeengi, Maluk, Ngombe, Bokila, and Kaam. Together these ethnic groups are known as the Kuba. This name was given to them by their southern neighbors, the Luba, and has been used since by Europeans. Traditionally, members of the Kuba Kingdom had no single name for themselves or their kingdom, but called themselves the "people of the king."

The many ethnic groups that make up the
Kuba share some cultural values that set them
apart from other neighboring peoples. For
example, they all trace family relationships
through the mother's side rather than the
father's. A Kuba boy is considered to be more
closely related to his mother's brother than to
his own father. Traditionally, he lives with his
mother and father until his father's death.
Then he joins the village of his mother's
brother.

But there are many differences between the
various Kuba groups. In the past each Kuba
group existed as a separate people. The
dominant ethnic group in the region was the
Boshongo, who united as many as twelve neighboring peoples into the Kuba Kingdom.

The Boshongo were never the majority in the
Kuba Kingdom. At the end of the 1800s, for
example, they made up only 43 percent of the
population. Since other ethnic groups were not
united, they were unable to oppose the domi-
nance of the Boshongo, who became the rulers
of all the Kuba. The current Kuba king, Kot
Rene, is the twenty-second ruler from the
Matoon Dynasty of the Boshongo people.

▼ NEIGHBORS ▼

The Kuba Kingdom has been influenced by
its neighbors yet has had a strong influence on

The Kuba king and the ceremonies of the court have always been the focus of Kuba society. Seen here is a previous Kuba king surrounded by attendants.

them. Neighboring peoples have sometimes been part of the kingdom and at other times existed outside of it. This is particularly true in the south of the Kuba Kingdom, where the border has always been open.

The Kuba have adopted, combined, and rearranged many aspects of neighboring cultures into their own. Many social practices, religious beliefs, and ceremonies are shared with other groups in this central African region. The Kuba court ceremonies, for example, are similar to those of the Kongo Kingdom.

The binding elements that unite the Kuba have always been the king and the court

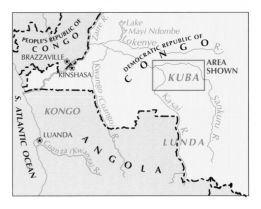

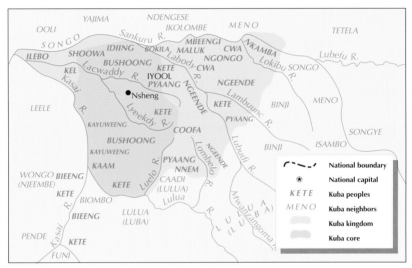

The many Kuba peoples live in the Congo. The Kuba royal capital is at Nsheng.

ceremonies of the capital city. Early European visitors were impressed by the highly organized capital. It had carefully planned plazas, as well as royal buildings that were enclosed by a ten-foot-high wall. The royal capital was the center of the kingdom, controlling the surrounding areas for about a hundred miles in every direction.

From early in their history, the Kuba maintained contact with African peoples who lived

The Kuba are famous for their weaving and embroidery. These women are embroidering woven cloth. The design on the left is called *djume nyimi*, meaning house of the king.

in faraway regions. Trade routes connected the Kuba Kingdom to the Pende and Lulua peoples in the south, the Luba and Songye in the east, the Ndengese in the north, and the Leele, Ding, and Kongo peoples in the west. The Kuba exported copper, ivory, and raffia cloth. They imported salt, cowry seashells, and pottery.

These relationships with distant peoples were not only important for the economy of the Kuba Kingdom, they sometimes affected cultural affairs, too. From the Kongo, for example, the Kuba borrowed certain weaving patterns and the board game known as *mancala* or *lyeel*.

13

▼ THE LAND ▼

The Kuba Kingdom is small, but unlike other, larger central African kingdoms founded around the same time (in the 1600s), it still exists today. The Kuba region in the Congo is now part of Kasai Occidental, a province, or state, that is smaller than the state of Connecticut in the United States.

Kuba territory is bounded on three sides by large and powerful branches of the Congo River: the Sankuru River to the north, the Kasai River to the west, and the Lulua River to the south. The eastern boundary is not as clearly defined. The few rivers within the Kuba region itself are the Lacwaadi, the Lyeekdy, and the Labody. These rivers, which provide good fishing and fertile soil for farming, contribute to the very high humidity of the area.

Dense tropical forests grow in the northern parts of Kuba country, where the rivers all flow toward the mighty Congo River. To the south, forests, lakes, and marshes give way to plateaus of bush and grasslands. Most of Kuba territory consists of gentle hills and valleys.

This equatorial region has one of the highest annual rainfall rates in the world. For nine months of the year there are frequent rains. However, the Kuba recognize four separate seasons: a short, somewhat dry period in January and February; a brief rainy season in March and

Most of Kuba territory consists of gentle hills and valleys. This party of men is walking in the vicinity of Nsheng.

April; a very hot and dry period from May to July; and another rainy season from October to December. The hottest part of the year is between June and November.

The Kuba are mainly subsistence farmers, meaning that they only grow the food they need to survive. Any surplus is sold at the market. Families grow bananas, corn, cereals, cassava, and root vegetables. Crops grown for profit include raffia palm and cotton, which was introduced during colonial times. Farmers also raise goats and sheep and keep chickens. Hunting, fishing, and trapping also provide food. In the past many animal parts, such as tusks and hides, were used in making fine costumes and art objects.▲

its own responsibilities. Traditionally, an official title is held for life. It cannot be passed to a son or daughter. However, if one male in a family gains high status, other family members may hope to benefit.

Kuba men who have earned royal privileges and high status proudly express their positions by owning certain important objects: bowls, cups, and pipes. The finer the craftsmanship and beauty of these art objects, the higher the social status of the owner.

▼ KUBA RELIGION ▼

Religious practice is focused on the king. Many royal ceremonies and complex royal symbols emphasize the religious importance of the king. The king's spiritual power played a

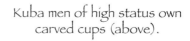

Kuba men of high status own carved cups (above).

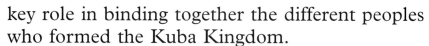

key role in binding together the different peoples who formed the Kuba Kingdom.

The Kuba traditionally believe that the king is a nature spirit, or *ngesh*. He represents the kingdom and has the greatest spiritual and worldly power of anyone in his realm. He is surrounded by his many wives and a court of people who serve him.

The *muyum*, the highest religious official, is responsible for all important religious ceremonies. Both the king's oldest son, who is called the *mwaaddy*, and the highest-ranking woman in the court must remember and pass on specific court knowledge, royal stories, and ceremonial rules to their successors.

The Kuba have at least seven different creation stories. These come from various Kuba chiefdoms that later united within the Kuba Kingdom. Although these creation stories differ in several respects, they all state that the world was created by either one or two gods, together with the first nature spirit.

The Kuba believe in a great number of nature spirits, which are identified with specific rocks, forests, or other features of the earth. Each village has a *ngesh* and usually a woman as its diviner—one who can see future events by interpreting dreams. Whenever there is trouble in the society, the spirit communicates with the diviner through her dreams, explaining the causes for

KUBA ORIGINS

Among the Kuba peoples, the most common creation story describes a Supreme Being called Mbwoom who created the first man, called Woot, and made him the first ruler of the earth. Mbwoom also made the first woman, Mweel, the sister of Woot.

All Kuba peoples are said to descend from Woot and are called the sons of Woot. Woot founded the Kuba peoples and began the first Kuba migration.

It is said that the original home of humans, including Woot, was beside the ocean. One day Woot contracted leprosy, a highly contagious disease. As a result, he had to leave the community. On his migration he was accompanied by his sister, Mweel. He left behind his wife, Pwoop, and his two sons, Ishwemy the elder and Nyimilwoong the younger. He went to live in a faraway forest with Mweel, where they had many children together.

Woot recovered from his leprosy and returned to his village. But the villagers had heard of Woot's incestuous relations with his sister, and they refused to accept him as their ruler. Once again, Woot was forced to leave.

On the night before leaving, Woot arranged for Ishwemy to succeed him as ruler. Woot promised Ishwemy that before his escape in the morning, he would hand over to Ishwemy all the king's regalia, including a leopard skin, an eagle feather, and other symbols of power that the king needed to rule. Woot told Ishwemy he would summon him with a special whistle the next morning.

A man from the neighboring Tshwa people overheard Woot's conversation with Ishwemy. The Tshwa man told Ishwemy to beware. He said that Woot really wanted to give Ishwemy his leprosy and not the kingdom. Then the Tshwa man reported what he had overheard to Woot's ambitious younger son, Nyimilwoong.

When Woot whistled the next day, Nyimilwoong came to his father instead of Ishwemy, who was too frightened. Woot, surprised to see his younger son, offered Nyimilwoong many fine clothes. Nyimilwoong demanded the royal regalia, threatening to prevent his father's escape. Woot had to agree. This is how Nyimilwoong became the founder of the Boshongo ethnic group. The title of king was passed down through his family line within the Boshongo people.

Woot fled with his wife, Pwoop, in a canoe and began the migration. Mweel tried to follow them, but they escaped by traveling far upstream and jumping from river to river.

Kuba diviners communicate with spirits by using this device, called *itombwa*. A diviner interprets messages from the spirits as she moves the small knob back and forth across the smooth top of the carving.

the upset and what the community must do to make amends. The welfare of the village depends on her communications with the *ngesh* and the prompt responses of the villagers.

According to the traditional Kuba view, a good person spends a short time after death as a ghost in the spirit world and then is reincarnated, or reborn. An evil person, however, cannot be reborn. He or she stays in limbo, the place between the worlds of the living and the dead.

Nature spirits and the spirits of dead people rarely cause harm. Misfortune is said to be caused by witchcraft and sorcery, however, which are combated by diviners.▲

chapter

3

HISTORY

THERE ARE TWO MAIN WAYS TO UNDERSTAND the Kuba past. The first is through Kuba oral history. This consists of historical knowledge and stories that have been passed down from generation to generation by word of mouth. Oral history accounts are often very complex and sometimes contradict each other.

The other way to understand Kuba history is through the research of scholars. These scholars include archaeologists, historians, art historians, language specialists, and ethnographers who study and compare ethnic groups. Some scholars also study the reports of early visitors among the Kuba, including traders, missionaries, and travelers. Most of these outsiders were Europeans. They admired the Kuba for their highly complex political system, the sophistication of their people, and their impressive judicial system.

WOOT'S MIGRATION

The stories of Woot's migration after he fled with his wife include many miraculous events. Mweel, his sister and former lover, chased after Woot and his wife. He performed many tricks to lose her. It is said that Woot took the sun with him when he left, leaving the whole world in darkness. Mweel sent messengers to him twice before he would return it. Woot is said to have taken many peoples with him. As they made their way upriver, several groups of these people decided to stop. They settled on the riverbanks and founded the first Kuba villages.

The migration stories describe numerous stages of Woot's journey. The stories name all the rivers and plains that Woot crossed and the villages he founded. Finally Woot and his followers reached their destination: the savanna of Iyool. They assembled on the vast plain of Iyool, around Lake Kum Idip. Among these early Kuba peoples were: the Bashibiyeeng under their chief, Shyaam Katudy; the Bangyeen under their chief, Mbeeny; the Bapyaang under their chief, Ibaan; and the Boshongo under their chief, Mboong.

One of these chiefs would become the *nyim*, or king of all the peoples in the region. To decide who would become king, a public test was proposed. Each chief would throw his anvil into the lake. The owner of the anvil that floated would become king and master of all the others. Mboong's anvil floated, and he became king. According to legend, this event was accompanied by other miracles. The waters of the lake reflected many colors; all of the trees bowed down to Mboong; and a crocodile tamely sat by the new ruler's side. Thus Mboong became the leading chief; he changed his name to Mantshu ma-Shyaang.

Only one chief, Shyaam Katudy of the Bashibiyeeng, did not accept Mantshu and declared war on him. Shyaam Katudy lost the war and Mantshu became the first king of the Kuba.

By combining information obtained from these two different approaches, we can understand a great deal about the Kuba past.

▼ ORAL HISTORY ▼

In the traditional Kuba view, history begins with the origin of the world. Every event in history is ordered according to which Kuba king was ruling at that particular time. The founder of many aspects of Kuba culture is Shyaam aMbul aNgoong, who ruled in the 1600s. His name was given to the palm tree from which palm oil is harvested. This oil plays a key role in Kuba society.

The Kuba term for history is *mooy ma walawal*, meaning words from long ago. There was no written historical record until the Kuba came in contact with other groups. Nonetheless, the Kuba have a strong sense of their own history, which they recount in songs and stories. These oral histories express the importance of kingship in Kuba culture and explain how the kingdom was formed. Most of the detailed stories describe the complex relationships of people in political and social groups, including the kingdom, the chiefdom, the village, and the clan.

These songs and stories of events and important people from the past have helped the Kuba make sense of the present. There are a vast number of oral traditions that speak of a rich, prosperous, and highly cultured people, proud of their origins and proud of their past. The Kuba attach great importance to their past. They view it as the force that has shaped their identity over the centuries and as the main source of their cultural pride today.

The Kuba Kingdom brought together a number of different peoples, each with their own oral traditions. Sometimes the oral histories of these different ethnic groups contradict each other over certain details. However, all versions are accepted as part of the important shared history of the Kuba. The differences between the oral accounts are used to explain different customs among the peoples who make up the Kuba Kingdom.

▼ KUBA KEEPERS OF HISTORY ▼

Certain members of the king's court ensure that tradition is respected, passed on, and maintained. They know the stories and songs and teach them to others. These court members who are the keepers of history include the king himself; the *muyum*, who is the head of important ceremonies of the kingdom; the *mwaaddy*, the king's eldest living son; and the woman whose task it is to teach the royal songs of the nature spirits to the king's wives. All are required to remember specific ceremonies and stories.

In addition, there are three other keepers of Kuba history: the *bulla*, the *chum* association, and the wives of the king.

▼ THE *BULLA* ▼

The guardian, or *bulla* (plural: *bulaam*), is a male official of the noble class. He recounts Kuba oral history and therefore has a deep understanding of both Kuba origins and society. The *bulla* is also the leading authority on Kuba dance and performance. He teaches dance and ensures that ceremonies are performed on the correct days of the Kuba religious calendar. By remembering the past of the Kuba and following the calendar of holy days, the *bulla* keeps Kuba culture alive.

Kuba oral history includes numerous lists of kings and officeholders, place names, and family lines dating back many generations. Knowing these by heart and understanding their relevance to Kuba history are the important tasks of the *bulla*. The Belgian anthropologist Jan Vansina reports that in the 1950s people greatly admired those *bulaam* who could recite this material.

▼ THE *CHUM* ASSOCIATION ▼

The eighteen councillors who serve the king make up the *chum* association, which determines the official history of the Kuba. The members undergo an initiation process. During this time,

Public dances (above) and court ceremonies are both important ways of celebrating and preserving Kuba tradition.

they hear accounts of the glorious past, important events, and the feats of great kings, especially the exploits of Shyaam aMbul aNgoong, the ruler credited with bringing unity to the kingdom.

Such in-depth knowledge of the past is reserved for certain people. The higher a noble's rank, the more he is allowed to know. Most ordinary people know much of this history, although in lesser detail. Oral history is passed from expert to learner.

▼ ROYAL WIVES ▼

The wives of the king are the third group of historians. They continue the oral tradition by

Women are also involved in the functioning of the Kuba court. The king's many wives are particularly important as keepers of history. Women's dances (above), like those of men, are a vital part of Kuba culture.

chanting verses of praise called the *ncyeem ingesh*, or songs of the nature spirits. They also sing verses that praise the royal family. Each king has a song dedicated to praising him. A special song praises all the kings' mothers by name. Other praise songs are more general.

The task of teaching these songs to the king's wives is given to a respected woman of the court. In order to teach them to others, she must memorize the chants exactly.

▼ PATTERNS OF HISTORY ▼

In addition to oral history, certain kinds of art, patterns, and objects also recall Kuba history.

Each Kuba king is credited with creating a particular pattern, such as the one seen here in the royal court.

Every Kuba king is credited with having invented a particular pattern. These patterns were used in the decoration of their royal palaces, in woven mats and fabrics, and in various carvings of wooden art objects. In everyday life, therefore, the pattern on a person's clothing may remind viewers of a particular king.

Kings are also associated with certain objects. The great Kuba king, Shyaam, is said to have introduced the board game called *lyeel*, which is

Seen here is the ceremonial costume of King Mbop Mbine. The shirt is made of raffia fiber and decorated with cowrie shells, fur, copper, and beads. This costume is now in the Newark Museum in New Jersey.

still played in honor of him. Another Kuba king, who ruled during the early 1900s, was shown a bicycle by some European visitors. He was so impressed by the pattern of the tire tracks that he used it to design a new fabric motif.

▼ MODERN SCHOLARS ▼

Modern scholars believe that the different Kuba accounts of their early histories suggest that the various Kuba peoples settled their territory over a very long period—about 2,000 years. This also might account for both the wide scattering and the complex mixture of peoples and cultures in the region. Excavations of historic sites in the Kuba region are just beginning. This archaeological research will certainly provide many answers to the story of the Kuba past.

However, from what we already know, the Kuba Kingdom began to emerge sometime between 1200 and 1500. Other great central African kingdoms were forming at this time: the Kongo, Luba, Lunda, and Mangbetu kingdoms.

In the 1500s the Kongo Kingdom on the Atlantic coast was invaded by the Jaga. Some experts believe that many of the people who later became Kuba were refugees from the Kongo Kingdom. They fled to the east to escape this unrest. These people established themselves between the Sankuru and Lulua rivers in an area bordered by the Luebo and Mweka Rivers to the south and the Ilebo River to the east.

The early Kuba Kingdom was reorganized in the 1600s under Shyaam, the first king of the Matoon Dynasty, and began to exert a strong influence on neighboring peoples. The kingdom reached its height of power in the 1700s and remained stable until the late 1800s. The kingdom's strength provided protection against outside slave raiders, who increasingly disrupted other central African communities in the 1800s. The Kuba Kingdom prospered during this time. Its people placed emphasis on hard work and on gaining wealth and status. Through intelligence

These men are important title holders at the royal court. They each have special costumes and weapons that indicate their status.

and hard work, any man could achieve an important position in Kuba society and even reach the level of the royal court.

▼ THE ROYAL CITY ▼

In the past the Kuba king himself unified the kingdom. The royal capital, Nsheng, with the king's palace at its heart, was the political, administrative, and economic center of the kingdom. It was also the cultural center where the

This view of Nsheng shows women grinding grain as male officials approach.

most impressive Kuba ceremonies and dances took place.

Between 5,000 and 10,000 people lived in Nsheng. The most important residents were the king, his wives and relatives, his court officials, and the Kuba nobles. Craftsmen, tailors, and sculptors, who lived in a special section of the city, were essential to the court. Important markets were located on the outskirts of the royal city, where traders from distant places came to do business.

When a ruler died, he was buried inside his palace. The king's oldest brother or one of his nephews from his mother's side of the family succeeded him. Once installed the new king immediately selected a new site on which to

Important markets, such as the one seen here, are located on the outskirts of the royal capital.

build his own personal palace. This then became the center of a new capital city. The royal capital was therefore always identified with the ruler who established it. In fact, all the royal capital cities have been established fairly close to each other, on a narrow strip of land less than twelve miles long at Nsheng.

Each new king named his capital with a shortened version of his own personal motto. The capital of King Kot aMbweeky III, for example, was officially named Ntsheminen at a public ceremony in September 1971. This place name is a short form of a Kuba saying that translates as "The community should discuss great problems, or else its children will suffer." This saying underlies the Kuba belief that a har-

CAPITAL CITIES

Royal capitals were designed by court architects. They based the capital layout on an east-west axis, since oral history records that the Kuba migration began in the west and moved east. The importance of this layout is also emphasized during royal masquerades and masked performances. The king begins his performance on the southwest side of the public square and moves to the northeast.

The capital is divided into northern and southern areas, each with an important noble as overseer. The king's personal apartments and the adjoining residence for the king's wives straddle the north-south dividing line. These buildings are located at the extreme western side of the capital, at the end of an open avenue that leads directly from the main entrance in the east. This layout ensures that the rising sun shines through the entrance and illuminates the palace.

monious political system, in which people are able to voice their opinions, best promotes the welfare of its people. At the ceremony, King Kot aMbweeky III announced that in the future, the Kuba capital would no longer move. Building a new capital has become impractical because of all the expensive systems that a modern town requires, such as electrical and water systems.▲

35

chapter

4
ART

KUBA ART IS NOW FAMOUS THROUGHOUT
the world, where it is displayed in many
museums. Kuba art objects associated with royalty and people of status are especially sought
after by collectors. These objects include fine
fabrics and carved wooden masks and drums.
Ornate objects carved from wood for daily
use—such as bowls, cups, spoons, pipes, tobacco
boxes, stools, and beds—are also prized by
collectors.

Kuba art is almost always decorated with
complex geometric patterns. Traditionally, it was
considered a great achievement to invent a new
pattern. Close to 200 designs are commonly
found today. Most are named after the men and
women who created them and have a certain
meaning. Some designs have more than one
name and meaning.

Kuba artists, such as those seen here, generally decorate the objects they make with rich and complex geometric patterns.

Every Kuba king had to create a pattern at the beginning of his reign. His pattern was displayed on his drum and, in the case of some kings, on a statue of the king.

▼ TEXTILES ▼

Early visitors to the Kuba region were particularly impressed with Kuba textiles made from raffia, a straw-like fiber. The fibers are pulled through a woven base and then cut, in much the

37

Kuba textiles, such as this raffia dance skirt, greatly impressed the first Europeans who visited the Kuba.

Men are responsible for all the stages in the preparation of raffia fiber. They weave it using a large wooden loom. Strung on the loom are all the long, vertical threads that form the base of the fabric, known as the warp. The weaver attaches thread to a shuttle and passes it back and forth between the warp threads, creating the shorter, horizontal threads of the fabric, known as the weft.

same way that many rugs are made. This technique, called cut-pile, creates a fine texture. European visitors began to call the textiles Kasai velvets after the Kasai Province of Congo where the Kuba live. These fine fabrics, generally under two square feet in size, are rich in pattern and color. Some experts believe that Kasai velvets may have been influenced by similar textiles made by the Kongo people, who lived 700 miles to the southwest of the Kuba region.

This beautiful *ncaka kot*, or dance skirt, consists of many separate pieces of textile joined together.

The Kuba also create *ncaka kot*, a long piece of ornamental cloth made from dyed raffia. On special occasions, women wear the *ncaka kot* wrapped several times around their waists, usually over plain undergarments. At funerals, these raffia skirts and overskirts not only adorn the corpse but are also worn by female relatives and friends who gather to celebrate the deceased's life.

Once the men have woven the raffia fabric for the *ncaka kot*, women make it into garments and add ornamental designs onto the basic cloth. They sew cutout shapes of dyed raffia cloth onto the cloth base—a technique known as appliqué. The appliquéd shapes, generally widely spaced, may then be embroidered with raffia thread that has been dyed black. The various shapes that are used each have names. For example, the circle is *idingadinga*, the tail of a dog is *ishina'mbua*, and leaves are called *dash*.

The embroidery on the various Kuba textiles of the 1700s and 1800s was more intricate than that found on later examples. It shares many designs with those seen on Kuba wood carvings and mats. The entire surface of the early textiles and wooden objects is densely covered with geometrical designs. These earlier examples are known as *buiin bu mishiing*, meaning designs sewn from strings.

▼ MASKS ▼

The Kuba king is the owner of three special types of masks that are used at royal ceremonies, initiation ceremonies, and funerals. On his behalf, palace officials strictly control how the masks and costumes are made and when and where they appear in public. Specific dances, songs, and instruments are associated with each mask.

Two types of masks, *mwaash aMbooy* and *ngady amwaash*, recall the story of Woot and his sister, Mweel. The *mwaash aMbooy* mask has the features of an old man with a white beard. It represents Woot and also the wise old men of the community who have great experience. At official ceremonies, the king wears this mask to emphasize both his royalty and his ties to the ancestral origins of the people. His mask is the model for similar masks worn by village chiefs when they are being honored by their people and when they are buried.

Ngady amwaash is associated with Woot's sister, Mweel. The face portion of the mask is decorated with many light and dark triangles and lines beneath the eyes, representing tears. The male dancers who wear it imitate women with graceful movements.

The third type of mask, *bwoom*, is large and has many decorations, including beads, hides, and cloth. In addition, sheets of metal are sometimes added to cover the forehead, cheeks, and

The *ngady amwaash* mask (above) is one of three royal masks. It is associated with Woot's sister, Mweel.

The *bwoom* mask (above) can be used to represent several different characters.

Today Kuba masks are on display in many of the world's museums. However, it is only when the masks are worn together with their full costumes (above) that the viewer can appreciate their full dramatic power.

mouth. The face of the mask has a bulging forehead and a big nose. It is used to represent several characters: a prince, a commoner, a member of the Tshwa ethnic group, or a rebel at the royal court. At any performance, the spectators must figure out which character and historical events the mask is portraying. Unlike *mwaash aMbooy*, the *bwoom* mask is not buried with its

45

owner. It is kept in the family as a symbol of continuity.

In some performances, *bwoom* and *mwaash aMbooy* compete for the affections of the female mask in the trio, *ngady amwaash*.

In addition to the three royal masks, approximately twenty other types of masks are created. Most of these, including the *ishyeen-imaalul* mask, are used by a special group, called the Babende association, during initiation ceremonies.

▼ *NDOP* FIGURES ▼

When a new Kuba king came to power, he ordered a sculptor to carve a statue of him, called a *ndop* figure. Only one *ndop* was carved for each king.

Ndop figures are generally between eighteen and twenty-two inches high. They were carved from *iloonc*, a hard, fine-grained wood. After carving, a protective coating of palm oil and camwood (a red powder) was applied.

Today only a few *ndop* figures survive of the 125 kings listed by oral historians. The five *ndop* that are considered the earliest surviving examples all show the ruler in a seated position. The heads of these five figures are enlarged in relation to the rest of the king's body. Scholars believe that they were carved in the mid-to-late 1700s, when the power of Kuba kings was increasing rapidly.

Each *ndop* represents a particular king, who is identified by a particular object associated with his reign. The *ndop* figure of King Shyaam aMbul aNgoong, for example, shows him holding the game board for *lyeel*, a game he is said to have introduced. Another king named Mbop Pelyeeng aNce promoted blacksmithing and is shown holding an anvil in Kuba artwork.

During the king's life his *ndop* served as his double. If the king was away from the court, the *ndop* served in his place. The statue was kept in the living quarters of the royal wives, who took care of the *ndop* as if it were the king himself. When a royal woman was about to give birth, the *ndop* was placed near her to ensure the safe delivery of the royal baby.

After the king's death, the *ndop* was stored away. However, on important occasions it was displayed as a way of remembering the dead king. This use of the *ndop* as a memory tool was remarked upon by King Shyaam in the early 1600s. He said about his people, "When they look at this statue, they will be able to remember me, and think that I watch over them, consoling them when they are sad, giving them inspiration and fresh courage."

In 1892 an African American Presbyterian missionary, William Sheppard, visited the palace of King Kot aMbweeky II. While he was in the company of the king, he witnessed four *ndop*

For many decades Kuba artists have carved *ndop* figures for sale to tourists and art collectors.

statues being placed on an earthen platform near the king. This unusual sight suggests that his visit was regarded as a very important event.

For many decades the Kuba have created copies of *ndop* figures for sale to tourists and art collectors.▲

chapter

5

COLONIALISM AND INDEPENDENCE

THE HISTORY OF THE KUBA AND OTHER peoples in the Congo has been greatly influenced by the colonial period. In the late 1800s several European countries, including Britain, France, Germany, Belgium, and Portugal, competed with each other to gain control over the rich resources of Africa. At the Berlin Conference (1884–1885), the European powers divided Africa into colonies, ruling them as their own possessions.

▼ KING LEOPOLD II OF BELGIUM ▼

A prominent figure at the Berlin Conference was Henry Stanley, an American explorer. In his extensive travels throughout Africa, Stanley followed the Congo River from its source to the sea. He received financial backing from King Leopold II of Belgium, who planned to claim an

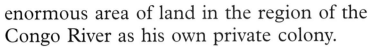

enormous area of land in the region of the Congo River as his own private colony.

Stanley aided Leopold's plans by signing treaties with many chiefs in the Congo, including the Kuba king. At the Berlin Conference, Stanley obtained American support for Leopold's planned colony, called the Congo Free State. The word "free" referred to Leopold's idea that businessmen from all over the world would be free to set up businesses in his colony. Stanley played a crucial role in making Leopold's colony a reality.

Leopold's rule of the Congo Free State was corrupt and brutal. Leopold made millions of dollars—and millions of Africans died as a result of his rule. Africans in his colony were forced to provide free labor and were terribly mistreated. Many were worked to death; others became refugees who died of starvation and disease. These events caused an international scandal, and in 1908 Leopold was forced to hand over control to the government of Belgium. His colony was renamed the Belgian Congo.

▼ THE BELGIAN CONGO ▼

Under Belgian control the Congo Free State was divided into fifteen districts. Each was overseen by a district commissioner who reported to the colony's governor-general. This system reduced, reorganized, or eliminated the authority of African rulers. It ignored the existing boundaries between African states and ethnic groups.

Under Belgian colonial rule, only some Kuba men who held high rank in the Kuba Kingdom were given administrative powers and a salary by the Belgians. However, Kuba of low rank who had adapted to Western ways often worked for the Belgians as salaried administrators. Many Kuba resented the fact that these new colonial authorities had risen to high office, bypassing the traditional Kuba routes for earning positions.

▼ RESISTANCE ▼

The Kuba's dissatisfaction with Belgian rule led them to participate in several general uprisings. These began in the Kivu region in 1903 and caused great civil unrest until 1908, after Leopold had handed control over to Belgium. Though these uprisings were crushed by the Belgians, resistance continued throughout the first half of the 1900s.

Resistance had very little impact on the colony's economy, which developed rapidly and made King Leopold II extremely wealthy. Neither under Leopold's rule nor under Belgian rule were the benefits of the economy passed on to the Kuba or the other African peoples who lived in the colony.

▼ INDEPENDENCE MOVEMENT ▼

Throughout Africa in the 1950s, Africans began to form political parties and demand their rights.

In 1950 a political organization called ABAKO (Alliance of the Kongo People) was formed in the Belgian Congo. ABAKO's main goal was to split away from the Belgian Congo and reestablish the great Kongo Kingdom as an independent country. After winning a municipal election in 1957, ABAKO's leader, Joseph Kasavubu, demanded general elections in the Belgian Congo and independence from Belgium. Other political groups throughout the colony made the same demands.

In January 1959, a riot erupted in Leopoldville after Belgian officials broke up an ABAKO rally. Colonial troops killed dozens and wounded more than 100 people. This incident, coupled with mounting political pressure against Belgian rule, convinced the Belgians that they could no longer prevent the local people from gaining independence.

In early 1960 the Belgian government held a large conference in Brussels with many African organizations present. It was decided that on June 30, 1960, the Belgian Congo would become independent and be renamed the Democratic Republic of the Congo. Joseph Kasavubu was named president. Patrice Lumumba, leader

The Congo was granted independence from Belgium in 1960. Seen here is a group of Kuba title holders together with a Belgian colonial officer (center).

of the Congo National Movement (MNC), became the new prime minister.

Shortly after independence, trouble broke out in Katanga, a mineral-rich and prosperous province of the country. The major political leader in this area was Moise Tshombe, head of a political party called CONACO (Convention Nationale Congolaise). CONACO followers—many of them white businessmen—believed they would be far better off if Katanga broke away from the rest of the country. When Katanga seceded in July 1960, civil war broke out. The newly independent country could not afford to lose Katanga and defeated the breakaway province.

53

▼ MOBUTU ▼

Over the next few years a new leader emerged: Joseph-Désiré Mobutu. He led an army coup that overthrew Prime Minister Lumumba and his government in 1960. Mobutu then became head of the military. It is widely believed that Mobutu had Lumumba murdered.

Five years later, Mobutu led a second coup to overthrow Tshombe, who had become prime minister. Mobutu had himself installed as prime minister in 1966 and made himself president the following year. He widened the scope of the president's powers to enable him to rule exactly as he pleased, no matter what government was in power.

Mobutu introduced a policy called national authenticity, which was designed to emphasize ethnic African identities. He "Africanized" place names. In 1971 the Congo was renamed Zaire. He changed his own name to Mobutu Sese Seko, or, more fully, Mobutu Sese Seko Kuku Ngbendu Wa Za Banga, which means "the all-powerful warrior who will go from conquest to conquest leaving fire in his wake."

Surrounded by loyal followers, Mobutu set up a corrupt and repressive regime, which was supported by the United States and other Western countries. For more than three decades he drained the country's wealth and increased his own. It is estimated that he stole between 4 and 5 billion dollars. Transportation and trade networks, including roads, railroads, river transport, and airports, fell apart because of neglect and mismanagement. As road and river travel to the Kuba region became more difficult, the region became more and more isolated.

After 1990 Mobutu's dictatorship met with increasing resistance both inside Zaire and in the international community. He announced in 1990 that he would allow democracy, but instead he began a crackdown on the media. He secluded himself in his extravagant palace in his home village far from the capital, Kinshasa, and in his various luxury mansions in Europe.

Several governments came to power and fell under Mobutu's presidency, but he remained in control of the country's finances, the media, and the military. Meanwhile ethnic conflicts flared, particularly in the Shaba Province (formerly known as Katanga) and on the Rwandan border. Millions of Zaireans fell victim to illness, particularly malaria and epidemics of AIDS and the Ebola virus. The situation in Zaire continued to worsen.

In 1993 the United States, Belgium, and France urged Mobutu to step down, but he refused to do so. African leaders and many of his own advisers made the same appeal, but Mobutu clung to power and to life. Mobutu was

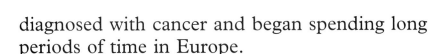

diagnosed with cancer and began spending long periods of time in Europe.

In October 1996, a rebel leader named Laurent Kabila launched a new campaign against Mobutu. Rebels in eastern Zaire, who were largely Zaireans from the Tutsi ethnic group, began to attack government forces and installations. During the ethnic conflicts between the Hutu and Tutsi groups in the neighboring countries of Rwanda and Burundi, Mobutu had supported the Hutu. Later he tried to expel Zaireans who were of Tutsi ethnic background and force them to go to Rwanda.

The rebels, assisted by Rwanda, quickly gained control of eastern Zaire. In March 1997, they captured Kisangani, Zaire's third-largest city. They encountered little resistance. Government troops, like most Zaireans, had lost all confidence in Mobutu and wanted to be rid of him. They were willing to surrender or join the rebels as they took over more and more of the country.

In May 1997 Mobutu was finally forced to step down. Laurent Kabila was appointed president, and the country returned to its earlier name of the Democratic Republic of the Congo.

▼ THE KUBA TODAY ▼

From the colonial era on, Kuba culture was greatly influenced by Western ways of life and economic systems.

Kuba children who live in rural areas, such as the boy seen here, often make their own toys.

Christian missionaries first came to the Kasai region in the 1870s and were established in the Kuba Kingdom by 1904. While some Kuba converted to Christianity, others continued to follow Kuba beliefs and blended them with some features of Christianity. Perhaps the missionaries' greatest impact was in providing elementary-level education to the Kuba and other ethnic groups throughout the country. In the 1970s the number of Kuba converts grew.

The Kuba Kingdom was made up of many different groups and encouraged individual achievement. These factors may have helped the Kuba adjust and succeed in the colonial era and in their multiethnic country.

Conditions in the Congo today are very poor. However, the royal capital of Nsheng, where these men are title holders, continues to be the center of the proud Kuba culture.

Mobutu left his country in ruins. Despite the bleak national situation in the Congo, the Kuba continue to take pride in their culture and their kingdom. Though many have left the Kuba area to follow their professions elsewhere, the Kuba royal capital of Nsheng continues to practice the court ceremonies and other cultural traditions that have developed over many centuries.

Those Kuba who remain in the royal capital live far away from the political centers of the modern Congo. This shields them from the violence and unrest of the cities. But they, too, suffer from the poor national levels of health, education, and food production. Their future, like those of all their fellow citizens, depends on radical improvements being made in the Congo.▲

Glossary

bulla (**plural:** *bulaam*) An oral historian and dance teacher.

bwoom A royal mask used to represent a variety of characters.

chum Advisers to the ruler.

coup Military overthrow of an established government.

diviner One who can foretell future events by interpreting dreams.

kolm An official of the court.

lyeel A game played on a wooden board. Also known as *mancala*.

Matoon The family name of the current Kuba royal family.

muyum Official in charge of court ceremonies.

mwaaddy The king's eldest son.

mwaash aMbooy A mask representing Woot.

ncaka kot Ornamental cloth.

ndop A carved wooden statue of a ruler.

ngady amwaash A mask representing a royal woman, usually associated with Woot's sister, Mweel.

ngesh A nature spirit.

nyim The king.

raffia Plant material from the raffia palm; it is woven into cloth.

For Further Reading

"Shyaam aMbul aNgoong." *Encyclopedia Africana Dictionary of African Biography II.* Algonac, MI: Reference Publications, 1979, p. 305.

Torday, Emile. *On the Trail of the Boshongo: An Account of a Remarkable and Hitherto Unknown African People*. New York: Negro Universities Press, 1969.

Challenging Reading

Adams, Monni. "Kuba Embroidered Cloth." *African Arts,* Vol. 12, 1978, pp. 24–39.

Meurant, Georges. *Shoowa Design: African Textiles from the Kingdom of Kuba*. London: Thames and Hudson, 1986.

Vansina, Jan. *The Children of Woot: A History of the Kuba People*. Madison, WI: University of Wisconsin Press, 1978.

———. "Ndop: Royal Statues Among the Kuba." *African Art and Leadership*, edited by Douglas Fraser and Herbert M. Cole. Madison, WI: University of Wisconsin Press, 1972.

Index

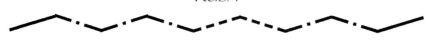

About the Author

Rebecca Leuchak studied African art at Columbia University and has worked with the collections of African art at the Metropolitan Museum of Art in New York City and the Musée Royale de l'Afrique Centrale in Belgium. She has taught African art at Hobart and William Smith Colleges, Connecticut College, and Wellesley College. She is currently teaching at Roger Williams University in Rhode Island.

Photo Credits

Cover, pp. 11, 15, 17, 27, 28, 29, 32, 33, 34, 37, 39, 43, 44, 45, 48, 53, 57, and 58 © Otto Lang/Corbis; pp. 8 and 13 © Eliot Elisofon Photographic Archives, National Museum of African Art; p. 18 (top) © Smithsonian Institute, Museum of African Art/Art Resource; p. 18 (bottom) © Werner Forman Archive/Art Resource, NY, courtesy of Entwistle Gallery, London; p. 21 © Aldo Tutino/Art Resource, NY, courtesy of National Museum of African Art, Smthsonian Institute; p. 30 © The Newark Museum/Art Resource, NY; pp. 38 and 40 © Werner Forman Archive/Art Resource, NY.

Consulting Editor and Layout

Gary N. van Wyk, Ph.D.

Series Design

Kim Sonsky